Animal Teeth

by Daniel Shepard

STECK-VAUGHN
A Harcourt Company

www.steck-vaughn.com

Some teeth bite and some teeth chew.

Teeth have many jobs to do!

Beavers have two big teeth.

Beavers use their teeth to cut down trees.

Sharks have many sharp teeth.

Sharks use their teeth to tear their food.

Horses have flat teeth.

Horses use their teeth to grind hay.

Some whales have tiny teeth.

Whales use their teeth to click and chatter.

Some snakes have teeth called fangs.

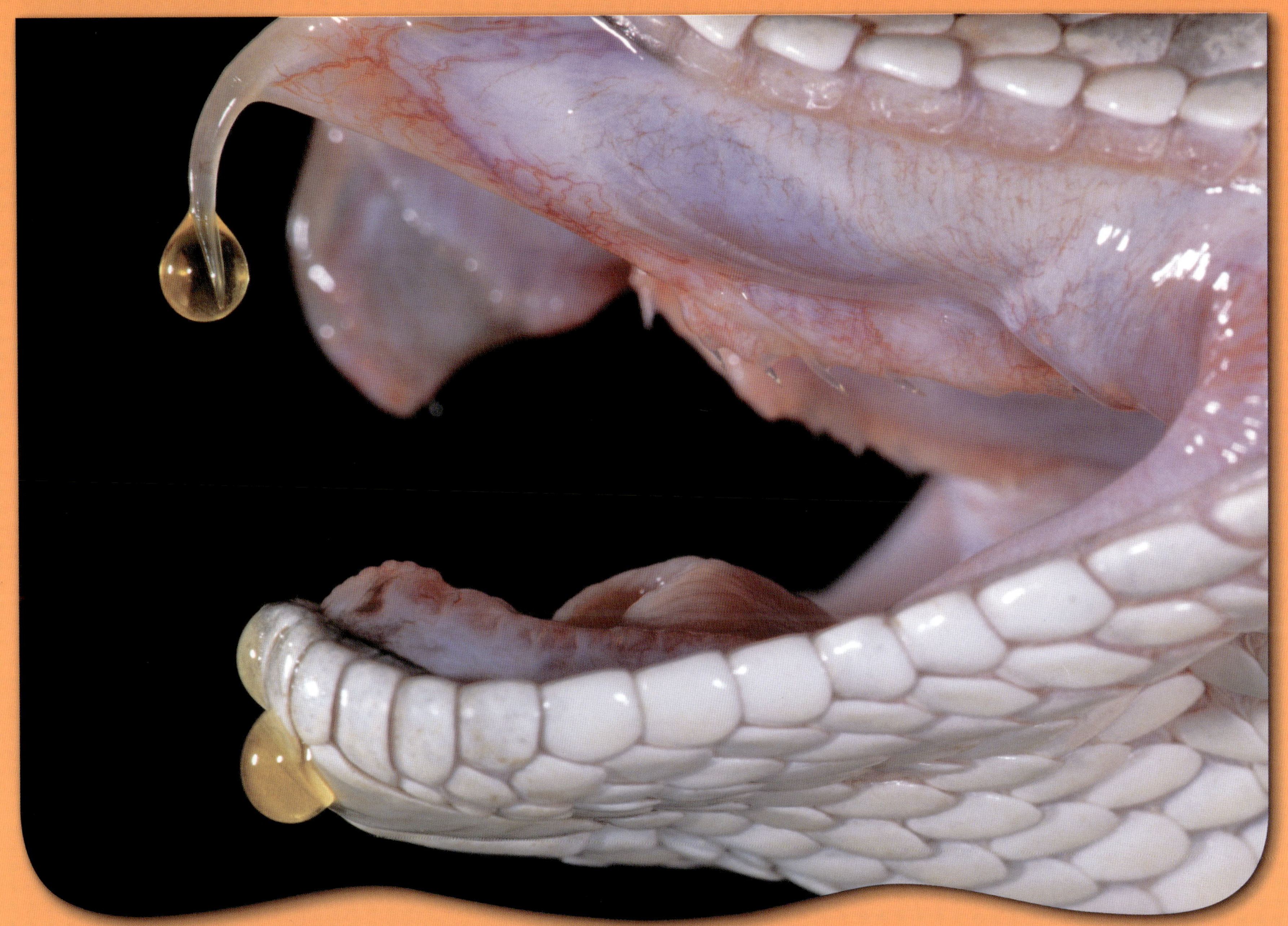

Snakes use their fangs to poison their prey.

Elephants have huge teeth called tusks.

Elephants use their tusks to dig for water.

This shrimp cleans the teeth of eels!